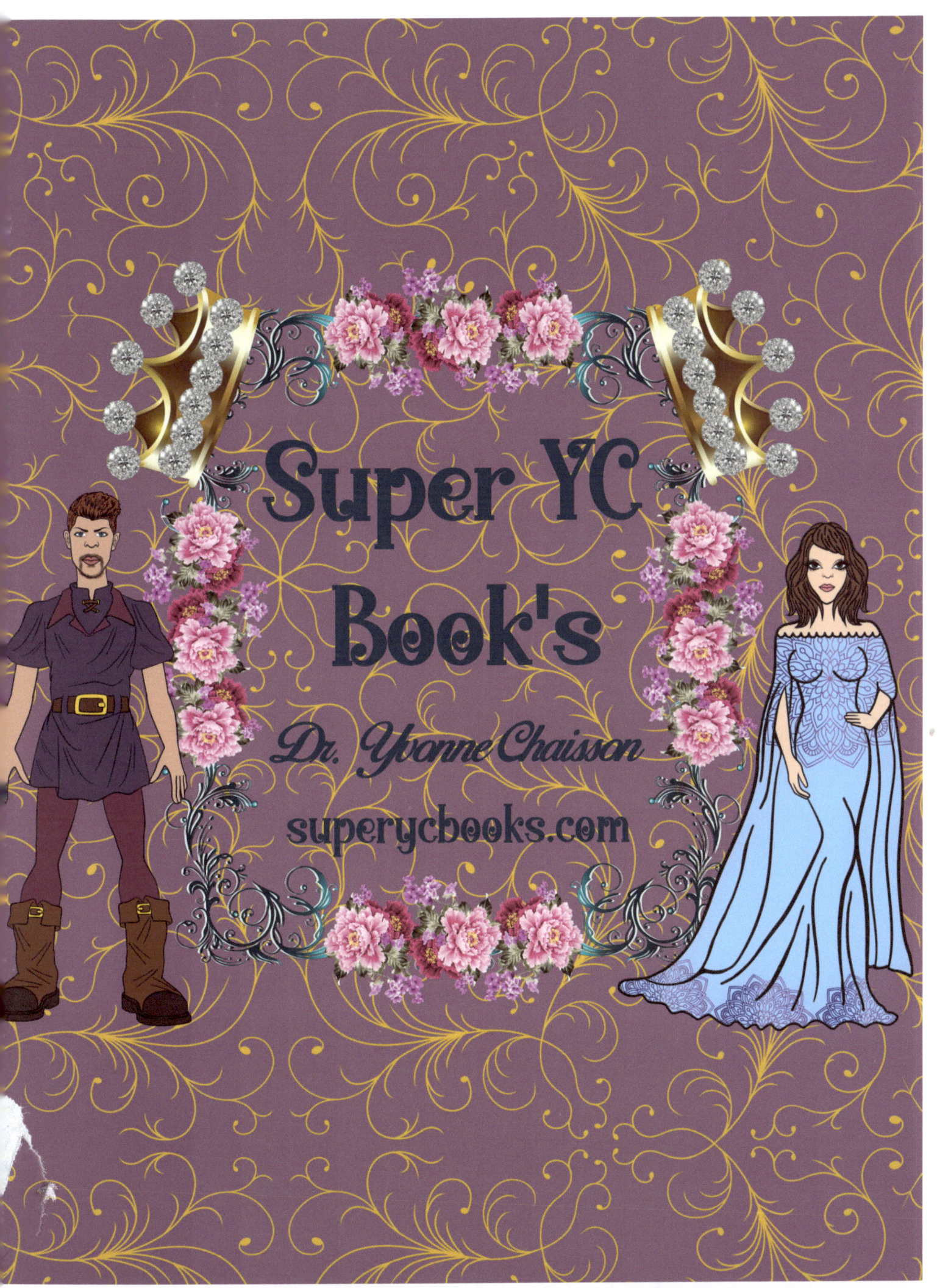

Text Copyright © 2021
Dr. Yvonne Chaisson
Illustrations Copyright © 2021
Dr. Yvonne Chaisson
Illustrations Copyright © 2021
Grady Chaisson
Published 2021
The rights of Dr. Yvonne Chaisson are to be identified
as the Author of this book.
The rights of Dr. Yvonne Chaisson and Grady Chaisson
is to be identified as the Illustrator of this book.
Copyright, Designs and Patents Act 1988
Text and Illustrations All rights reserved.
This book and or parts thereof may not be reproduced in any form.
Stored in any retrieval system or transmitted in
any form by any means electronic,
mechanical photocopy, recording, or otherwise.
Without prior written permission of the Author,

Except as provided by
United States of America copyright law

Super YC Book's - The Queen's Crown

Print ISBN 978-0-578-84897-6
Ebook ISBN 978-0-578-84899-0

Book Dedication

To my King Grady
Thank You

For your Loving words of Encouragement

For telling me I am Beautiful everyday

Grady you are my one and only for
35+ Years and counting

I LOVE YOU

Around the World & Back Again

Love Your Queen Yvonne

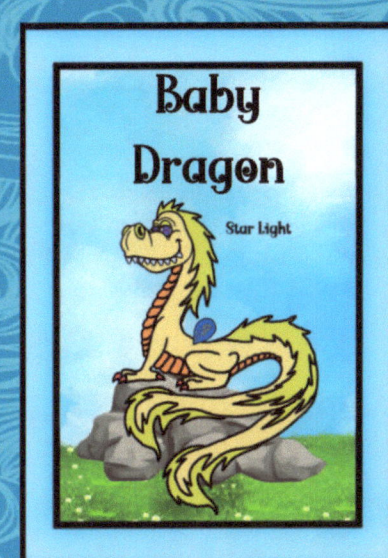

To see Queen Yvonne, they all said.

So now they all Hurried
off to see the Queen Yvonne

As they came to the Castle gates
Dotted Darnell was standing there.

Where are all of you
going in such a hurry?
said Dotted Darnell

We are going to see Queen Yvonne so we can show her all the new flower crowns that we made today!!! said Violet

I see said Dotted Darnell,
I think you all must have been in the
Queen's garden getting her flowers!!!

There comes
the King and Queen now
said Dotted Darnell

Yes, ma'am they are from your garden.
Your garden has the most
beautiful flowers of all the land
said Violet

May I ask you where
you got your Crown from Queen Yvonne?
Asked Wildflower

Yes, you may
said Queen Yvonne

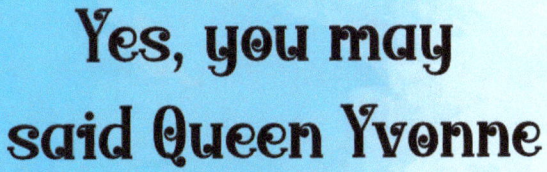

King Grady had our crowns made at Mr. Smith shop said Queen Yvonne

He made them so everyone would know that we were the King and Queen, said King Grady

Both of you watch over all of the lands and Kingdom so that we can all be one big happy family said Star Light

Official Art Drawing Contest Winner

We would like to say Thank You to all the boys & girls that enter the drawing contest at
Cheeseburger Bobby's in
Canton, Georgia.
The Winner is
Emily Smith Age-10
We would also like to say Thank You to
Jessica Johnson, Lawrence and Krista
for all their help.

Emily Smith
You are an Amazing young lady
So glad that we got to meet

Hello kids!

Did you know we have an

official Fan Club
and
official Birthday Club

You can join our Clubs
By sending us a letter and or a drawing
with a self-address stamped envelope.
Please include your name and age.
Your letter or drawing might be
featured in one of our books
We will send you a letter back with an
Awesome Surprise.

Send Letters Too

Super YC Book's
c/o Yvonne Chaisson
P.O. Box- 211
East Ellijay, Georgia 30539

Fan Club Wall Of Art

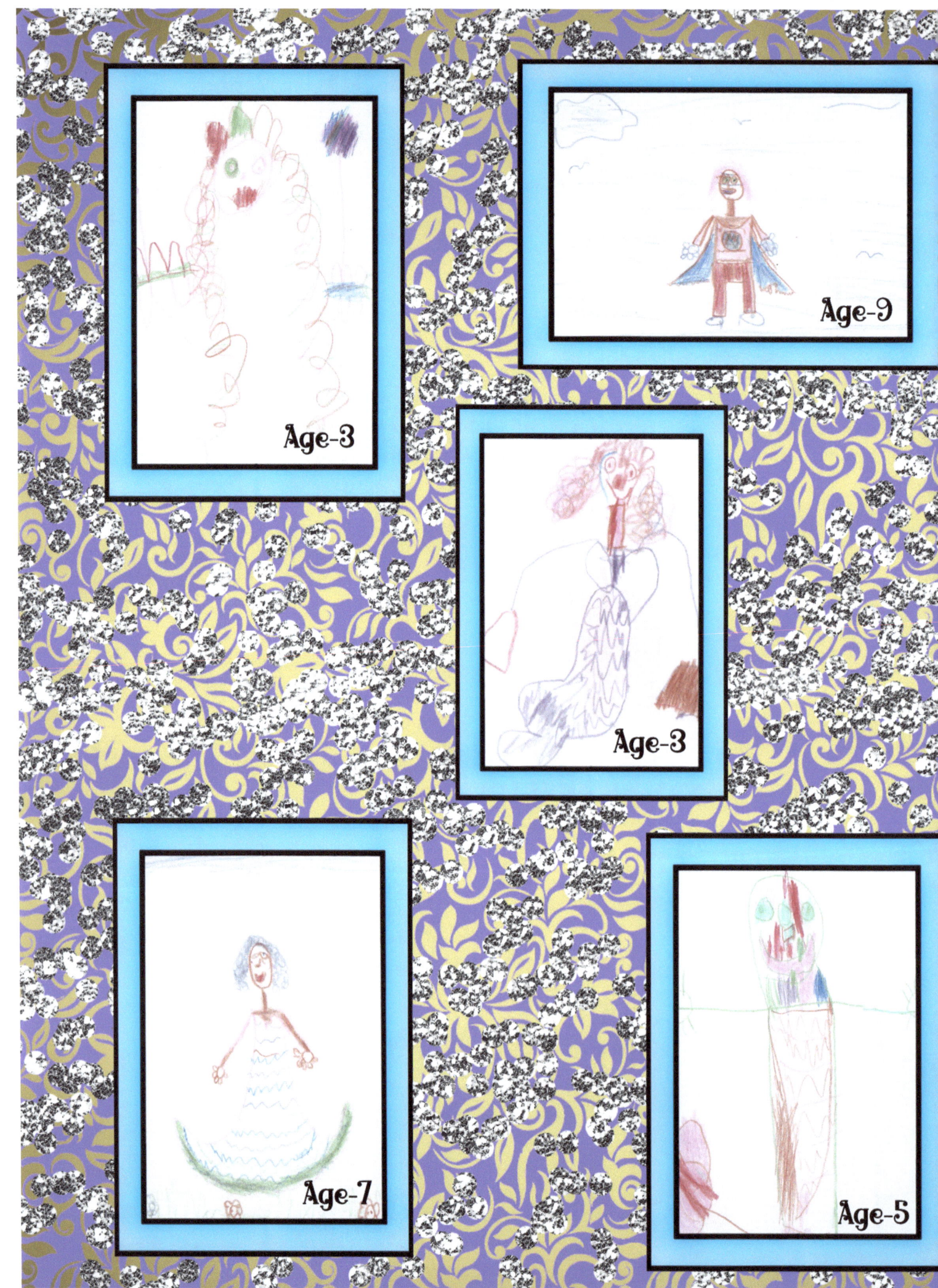

About Me

My name is Dr. Yvonne Chaisson

I am a Published Author & Illustrator
of two children's books Series.
Super YC Chearleene's Adventure book
&
Super YC Book's

I started writing & drawing in my journal in my free time.
Hoping to one day get my journals published.
10 years later

Published Author & Illustrators on
The New York Times Bestsellers List
With two Awards
Book Legacy Award 2020
&
Author Illustrator of The Year 2020

Thank You to all our Fans.

If you would like to know more
superycbooks.com

www.ingramcontent.com/pod-product-compliance
Lightning Source LLC
Chambersburg PA
CBHW041411160426
42811CB00106B/1667